MR BIG

A play written and illustrated by Ed Vere
Based on the original picture book

Characters

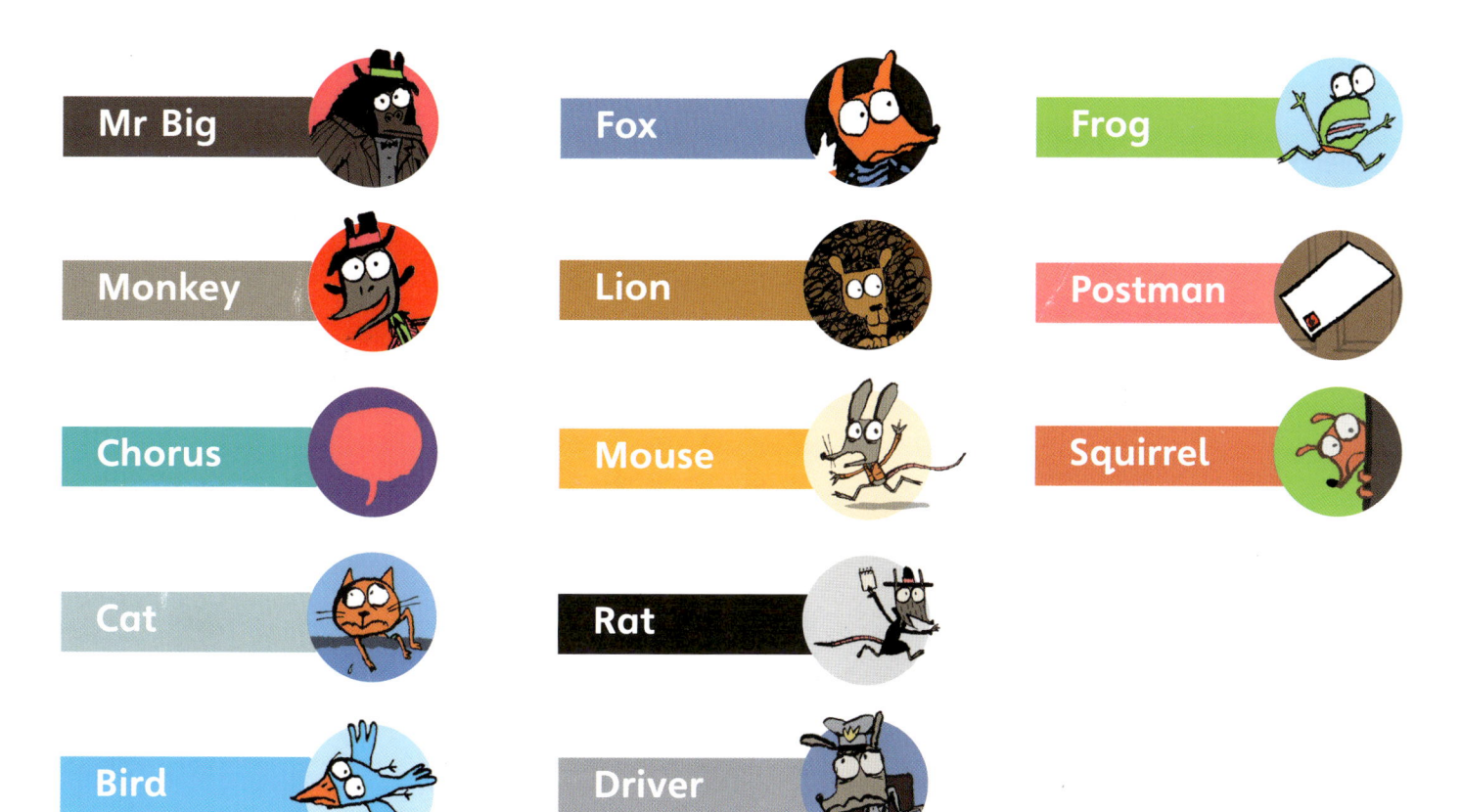

Mr Big	Fox	Frog
Monkey	Lion	Postman
Chorus	Mouse	Squirrel
Cat	Rat	
Bird	Driver	

Monkey: Let me tell you a story about a friend of mine.
He goes by the name of Big ...
Mr Big!
Now, Mr Big had a small problem.
Compared to everyone else, he was extremely ...
BIG!

Chorus: Big? He's not BIG,
he's BIGGER than BIG,
BIGGER than a BIG THING –
he's ENORMOUS!

Enter Mr Big.

Mr Big: Ahhh, what a beautiful day!
The sun's out and the birds are tweeting.
I wish I had someone to share it with ...

He walks to the park bench and sits down sadly.

Monkey: He was so big that everywhere he went,
all everyone saw was someone big and scary.

Chorus: Help! Look how BIG Mr Big is!
He sure is scary!

Squirrel hops by, picking up nuts along the way.

Mr Big: Hi, Miss Squirrel!
Will you sit down and chat with me a while?

Squirrel: Er ... h-h-hello, Mr Big! Sorry, I can't stop
– I've got nuts to collect! Must dash, there's
an acorn with my name on it!

Squirrel runs off.

Fox whizzes by on his skateboard.

Mr Big: Nice day for skateboarding, Mr Fox! Can I have a go?

Fox: Um ... Sorry, Mr Big! I've got an urgent appointment with ... er ... a chicken! I must skedaddle!

Mr Big: Oh well, I'd probably just have squashed his skateboard anyway.

Bird flies by.

Bird: Yikes! There's Mr Big! What if he sees me? Maybe I won't sing my song in that tree after all. Tweet you later.

Bird flies off. Mr Big sighs and gets up from the bench. He walks off.

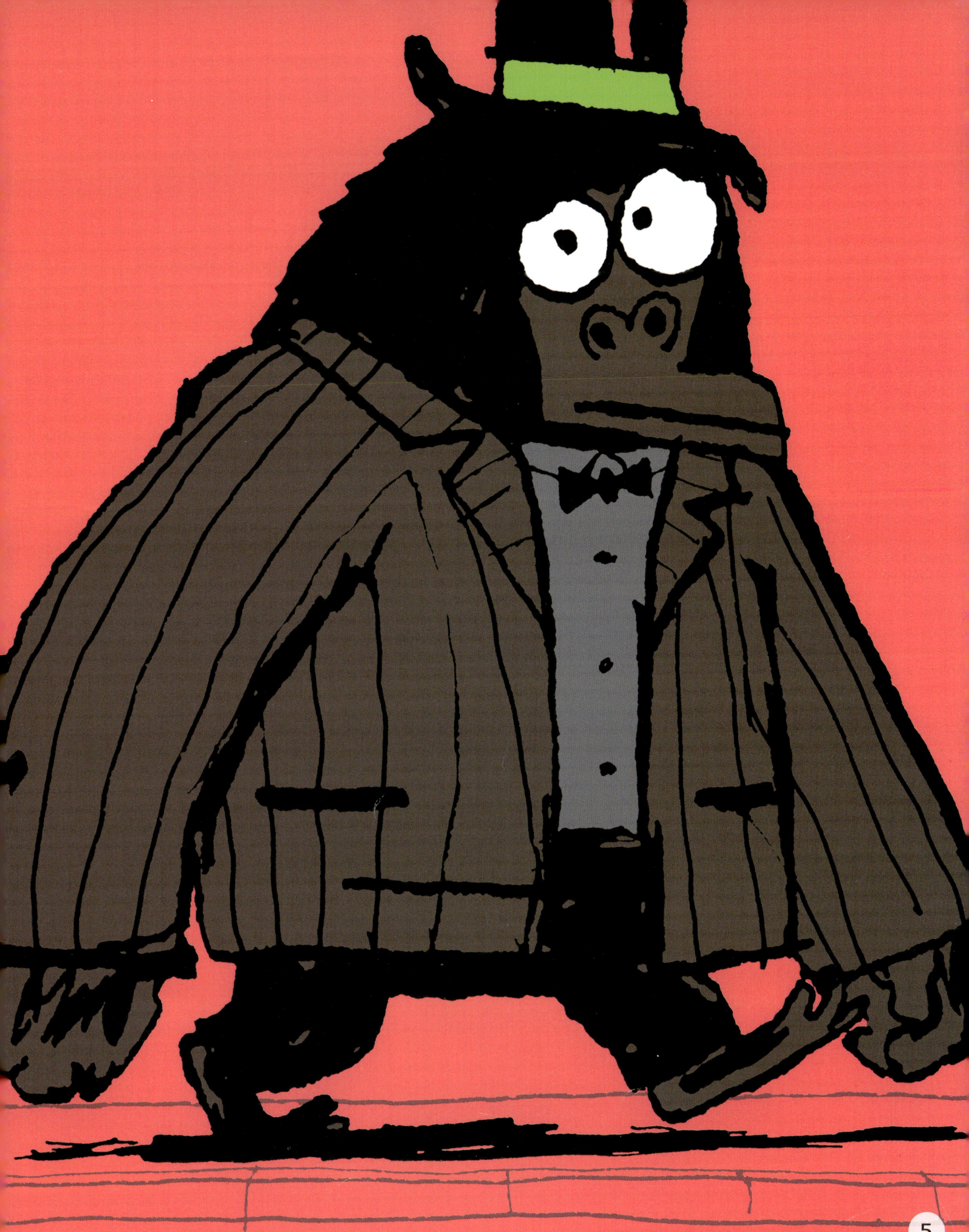

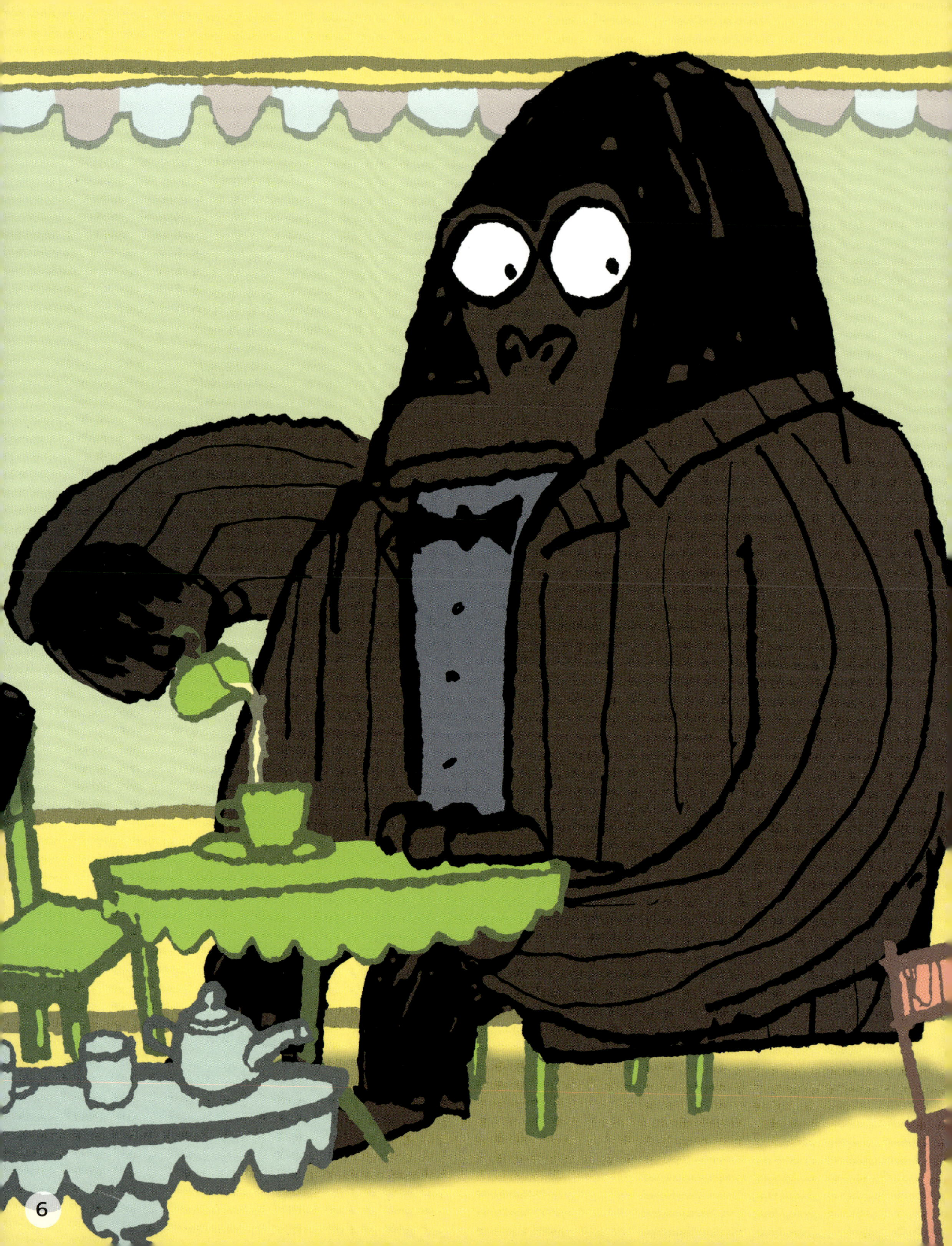

Monkey: No one stuck around to find out who he really was.
So inside, Mr Big felt very, very small.
And that's how it always was ...
One day, Mr Big went to the café.

Mr Big walks on and goes up to a café table where Rat is sitting.

Mr Big: Excuse me good sir, do you mind if I sit here?

Rat: Er ... GULP! Sure buddy, sit down!
I was just about to leave anyway!
I've got a bus to chase!

Rat dashes off, looking round nervously at Mr Big.

Mr Big: Well, it would have been nice to chat,
as it's been so very long since I've spoken
to anyone.
But that's okay, I probably would have bored
him anyway.
I'll just sit and hum a tune instead.

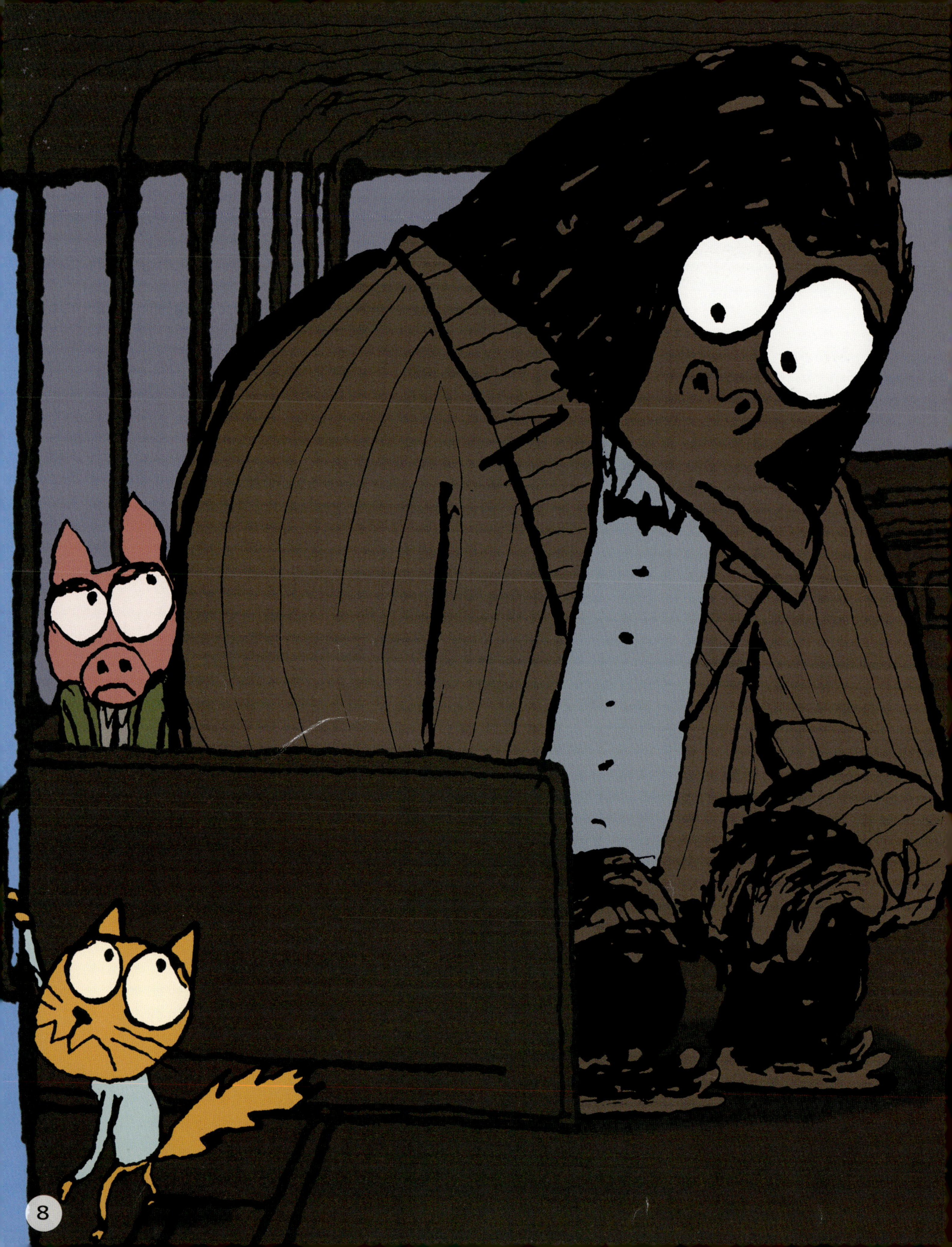

Monkey: And when Mr Big got on the bus,
well, what a surprise – everybody else got off.

Mr Big chooses a seat on the bus and sits down. Cat and Mouse rush down the aisle.

Mouse: Squeak – it's my stop!
Toodle-loo Mr Big – sorry I can't stay and chat!

Cat: Er ... yes, bye, Mr Big! I've got to hop off too ...
that mouse has my name on it!

Driver: Gulp ... Looks like it's just you and me, Mr Big.
Jeepers Creepers – is that the time?
It seems we've reached the end of the line ...
all change please, ding ding!!!

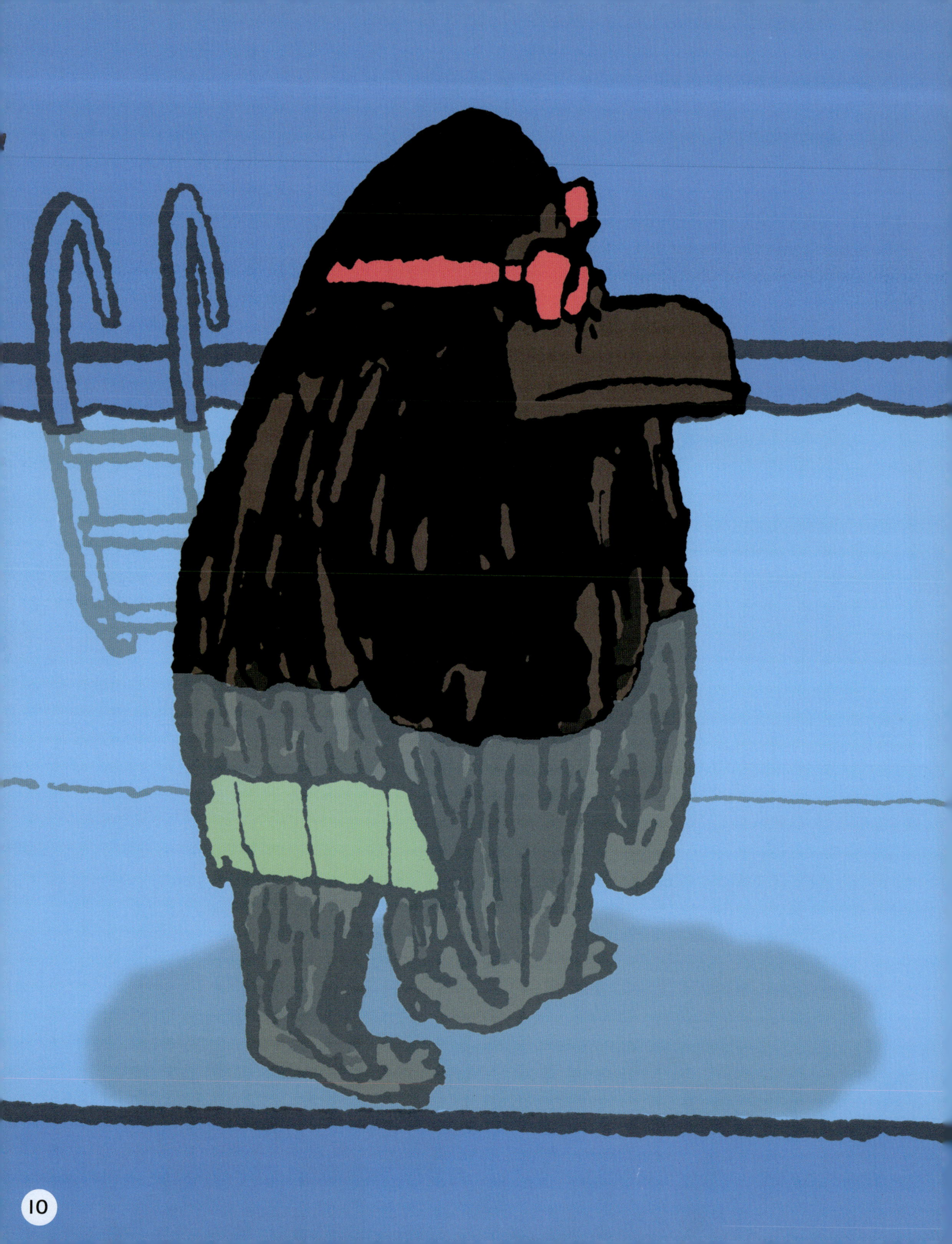

Chorus: Got to go! Got no time for poor old Mr Big!

Mr Big: Oh well – it's a nice hot day for a walk,
maybe I'll go over to the pool for a little swim ...
and maybe I'll treat myself to a nice cold banana!

Mr Big walks off.

Monkey: And when he got to the pool,
well, let's just say, everyone needed to be ...
somewhere else.

Mr Big enters wearing swimming goggles. He stands by the side of the pool, as if ready to dive in.

Frog: Ribbit! Ribbit!
Watch out!
He is enormous!
Let's get out of here before he squashes us like pancakes!
So long, Mr Big!!

Cat: Miaowzers, run for cover, he's going in!

Chorus: Wowsers, look who's coming,
get out of the way of poor old Mr Big!

Frog and Cat run off, followed slowly and sadly by Mr Big.

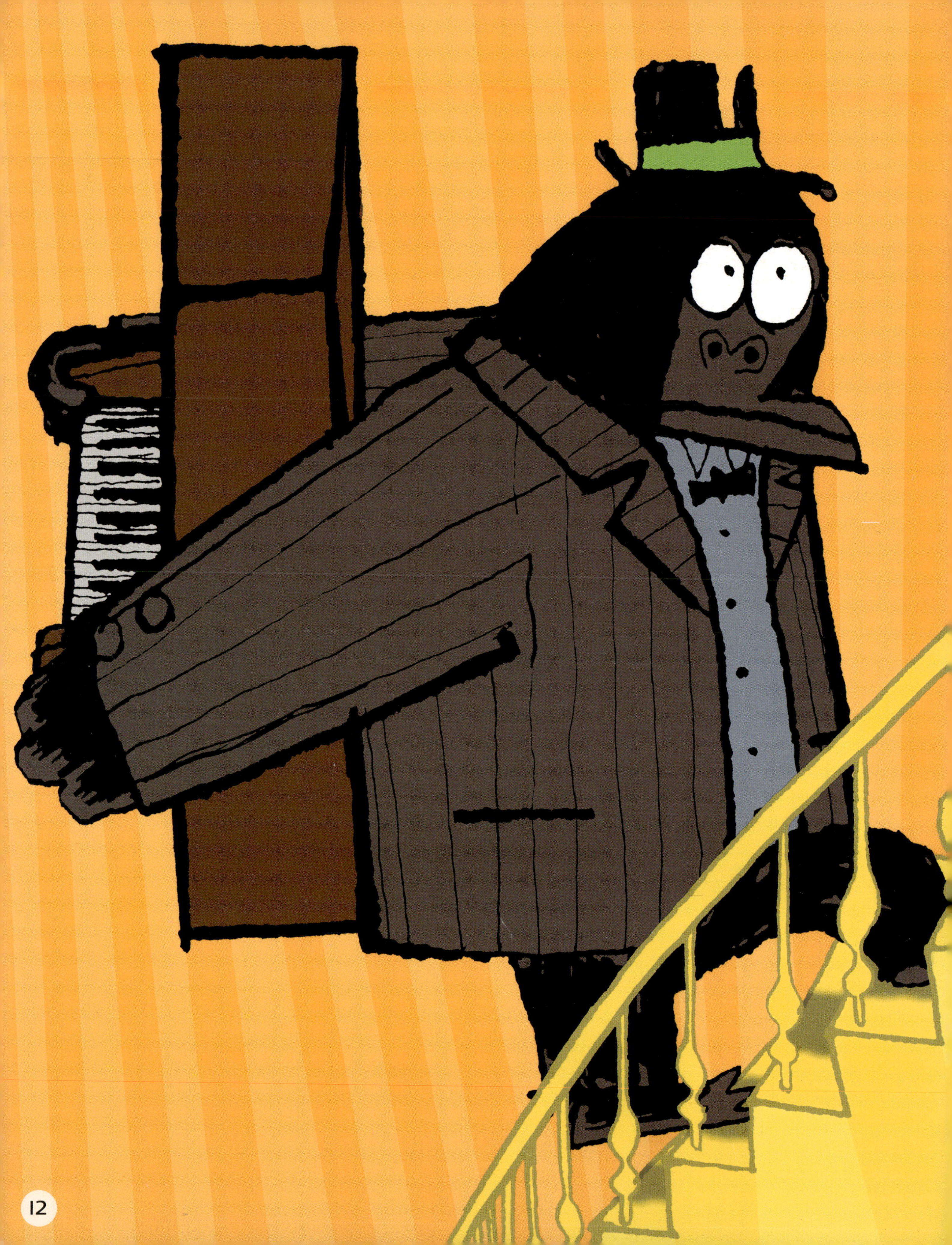

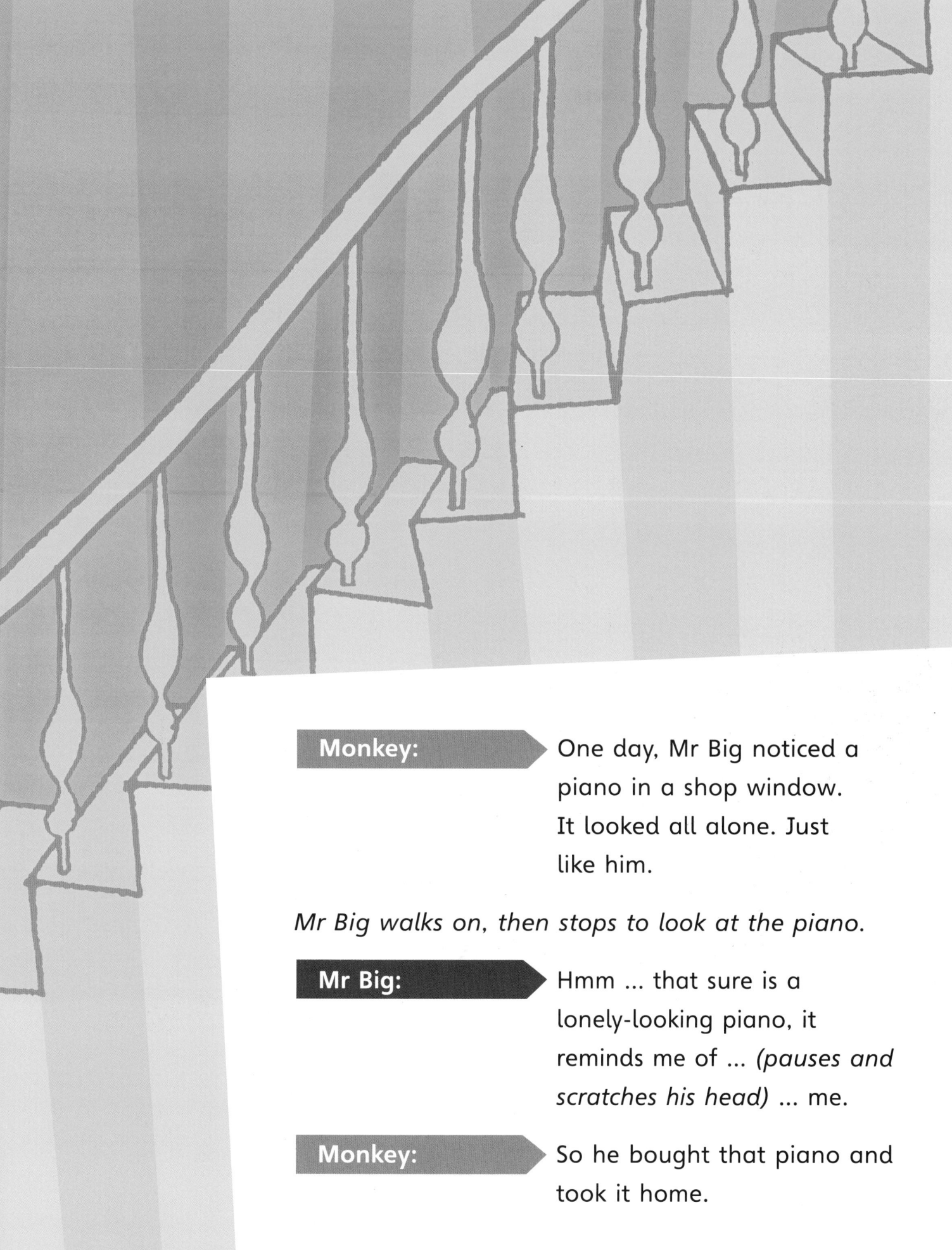

Monkey: One day, Mr Big noticed a piano in a shop window. It looked all alone. Just like him.

Mr Big walks on, then stops to look at the piano.

Mr Big: Hmm ... that sure is a lonely-looking piano, it reminds me of ... *(pauses and scratches his head)* ... me.

Monkey: So he bought that piano and took it home.

Mr Big walks slowly over to the piano and sits down. He sighs.

Monkey: As Mr Big sat alone at the piano,
he thought of all the things that made him sad.
And then he played.

Mr Big sits at the piano and sings this song in a slow blues style.

Mr Big: I'm lonely, I'm blue,
my heart's heavy too.
No one comes near me, dear piano ...
I walk the streets alone,
no need to use a phone.
No one to talk to, dear piano ...
Who is it people see?
It's not the re-al me.
Can you hear this, dear piano?
I know that I need a friend,
my broken heart to mend.
Until then I have you, dearest piano.

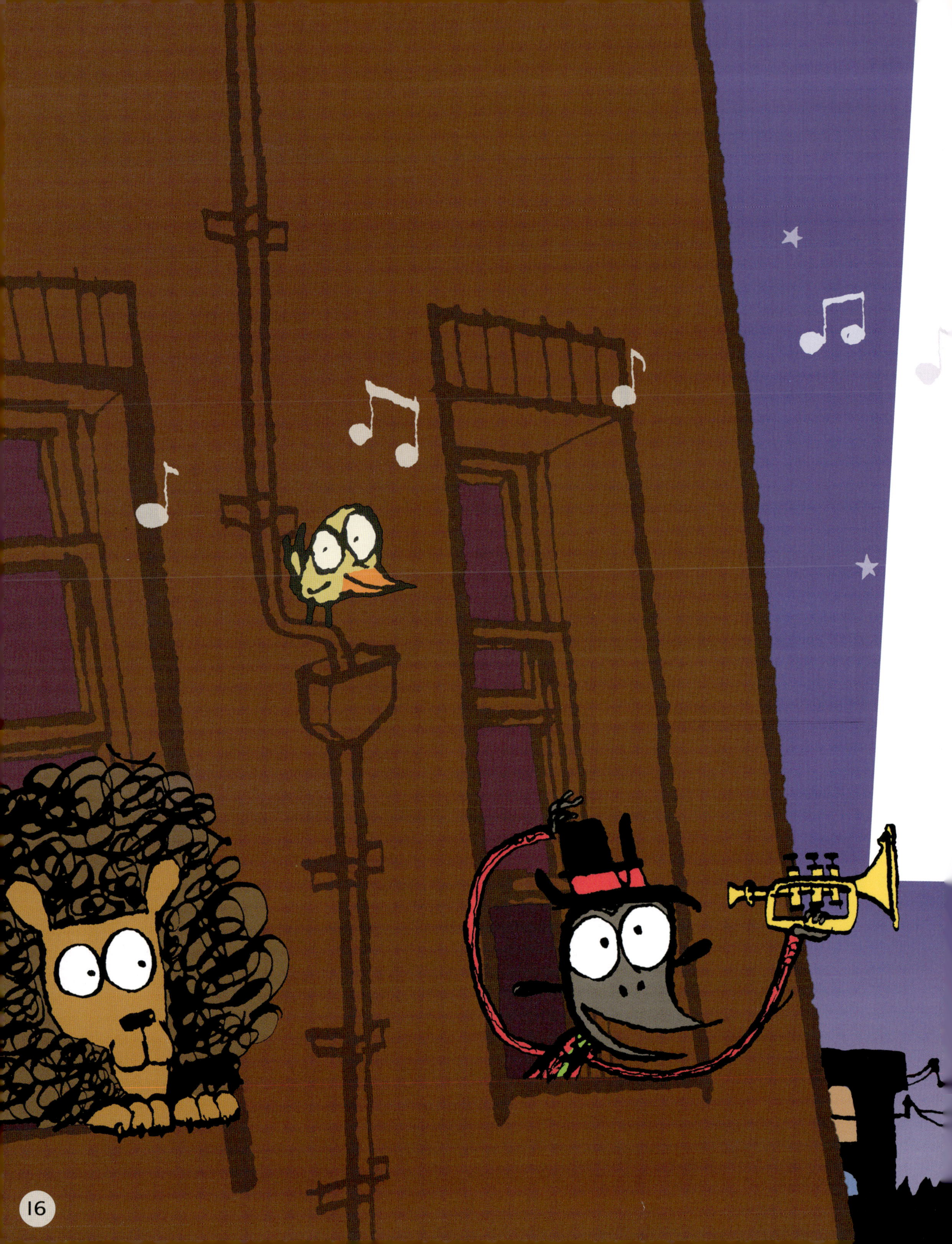

Monkey: His music drifted out through the open window and into the evening sky. It drifted across the rooftops, over to his neighbours.

Lion: Yo dude, who's playing that beautiful music?

Bird: Man, that cat can play!

Lion: That doesn't sound like a cat to me, baby!

Monkey: The word spread, and night after night everyone came from all over town.
And still no one knew who was playing.
It was a big mystery.

Chorus: Oooooo, BIG mystery,
who can it be?
Is it you?
I know it's not me!

Monkey: But inside, Mr Big was still alone.

Mr Big sits sadly at the piano, playing his sad tune over and over again.

Monkey: And then, one morning,
Mr Big received his first ever letter.

The postman tiptoes up and drops the letter on Mr Big's mat.
He whispers to the audience ...

Postman: Ssssshhhh, now hush up,
I don't want Mr Big to hear me!

Mr Big inspects the letter – what could it be?

Mr Big: It's addressed to 'The Pianist'!
Does that mean me?
Who'd write to little, I mean BIG old Mr Big?
Maybe it's a bill?
I suppose I should open it to see what's inside!

He reads the letter.

Dear Mystery Pianist,

Thank you for your ~~funky~~ beautiful music. Everyone's been listening to you for weeks, and we're all wondering ~~like~~ one thing... who are you? We'd love to meet you!

Me and a couple of the guys are ~~jam~~ playing tonight at the ~~four~~ Blue Note. Please come and join our band!

See you later?

A friend.

20

Monkey: That night, my friends, Mr Big joined the band. All night long the joint was jumping and nobody wanted to leave!
At last, everyone could see the real Mr Big.

Mr Big is playing the piano on stage and singing. Lion, Rat and Monkey are joining in. The audience watching the play also joins in.

Mr Big: Put your hands up people,
put your hands up in the air.
Wave them around
like you just don't care.
Clap your hands people,
clap your hands up in the air.
I'm so happy now
that I got new friends to share.
I'm going to sing a scat,
I'm going to sing a scat.
Do you know where that's at,
if I sing a jazz scat?

Mr Big: Listen up Daddio,
then repeat after me ...
B'doo B'daa B'daa,
B'doo B'daa B'dee!

Groovy man!

Audience repeats.

Mr Big: B'doo B'daa B'daa B'doo B'daa B'dee!

Audience repeats.

Mr Big: B'daa B'dee B'doo B'daa B'dee B'doo – Beep!

Audience repeats.

Mr Big: Beep Beep, B'daa b'daa, Beep beep b'daa.

Audience repeats.

Mr Big: Beep Beep b'diddley beep, b'diddley dada da doo.

Audience repeats.

Mr Big: B'diddley diddley doo B'daddily daddily daa –
B'doo B'dee B'doo B'dee B'doo B'dee B'daaa!

Audience repeats.

Mr Big: That was fun people,
let's go round again ...
B'doo B'daa B'dee B'doo B'daa B'dee!

Hot man!

Audience repeats.

Mr Big: B'daa B'dee B'doo B'daa B'dee B'doo – Beep!

Audience repeats.

Mr Big: Beep Beep, B'daa b'daa, Beep beep b'daa.

Audience repeats.

Mr Big: Beep Beep b'diddley beep, b'diddley dada da doo.

Audience repeats.

Mr Big: B'diddlley diddley doo B'daddily daddily daa –
B'doo B'dee B'doo B'dee B'doo B'dee B'daaa!

Audience repeats.

Mr Big: Yeah baby, that's where it's at
when Mr B is happy
and singing jazz scat!

Chorus: Wooooooo, yeah!!
Let's hear it for Mr Big!
Go, baby, go!
Groovy, man!
Yeah, Mr Big sure is cool!
He's cooking, Daddio!
Yeah, baby – jazz!

Monkey: Now that the Big Band has hit the big time and
everyone wants to meet them,
Mr Big has a new problem ...

GO BABY GO!!

Yeah cool!

That's all folks!

Mr Big:	Hey, guys, what's going down?!
Cat:	Please can you sign my book, Mr Big?
Rat:	Groovy, baby! I'm your biggest fan!
Mouse:	Er … squeak … is it really you?
Fox:	B'dee B'dee B'daa B'daa B'dee B'daa B'doo!
Monkey:	He doesn't get much time to be alone … and that's just the way he likes it!
Mr Big:	Yeah baby, being big ain't so bad after all!